W9-AZA-014

SUPER SIMPLE DIY

MAKE A ROBO PET

YOUR WAY!

Rachael L. Thomas

Consulting Editor, Diane Craig,
M.A./Reading Specialist

Super Sandcastle

An Imprint of Abdo Publishing
abdobooks.com

abdobooks.com

Published by Abdo Publishing, a division of ABDO, PO Box 398166, Minneapolis, Minnesota 55439. Copyright © 2019 by Abdo Consulting Group, Inc. International copyrights reserved in all countries. No part of this book may be reproduced in any form without written permission from the publisher. Super SandCastle™ is a trademark and logo of Abdo Publishing.

Printed in the United States of America, North Mankato, Minnesota
102018
012019

THIS BOOK CONTAINS RECYCLED MATERIALS

Design: Sarah DeYoung, Mighty Media, Inc.
Production: Mighty Media, Inc.
Editor: Megan Borgert-Spaniol
Content Consultant: Benjamin J. Garner
Cover Photographs: iStockphoto; Shutterstock
Interior Photographs: AP Images; iStockphoto; Paul Hudson/Flickr; Shutterstock

The following manufacturers/names appearing in this book are trademarks: Duracell®, Elmer's®, WowWee® CHiP™

Library of Congress Control Number: 2018948794

Publisher's Cataloging-in-Publication Data
Names: Thomas, Rachael L., author.
Title: Make a robo pet your way! / by Rachael L. Thomas.
Description: Minneapolis, Minnesota : Abdo Publishing, 2019 | Series: Super simple DIY
Identifiers: ISBN 9781532117190 (lib. bdg.) | ISBN 9781532170058 (ebook)
Subjects: LCSH: Robotic pets--Juvenile literature. | Handicraft--Juvenile literature. | Creative activities and seat work--Juvenile literature.
Classification: DDC 680--dc23

Super SandCastle™ books are created by a team of professional educators, reading specialists, and content developers around five essential components—phonemic awareness, phonics, vocabulary, text comprehension, and fluency—to assist young readers as they develop reading skills and strategies and increase their general knowledge. All books are written, reviewed, and leveled for guided reading and early reading intervention programs for use in shared, guided, and independent reading and writing activities to support a balanced approach to literacy instruction.

TO ADULT HELPERS

The projects in this book are fun and simple. There are just a few things to remember to keep kids safe. Some projects may use sharp or hot objects. Also, kids may be using messy supplies. Make sure they protect their clothes and work surfaces. Be ready to offer guidance during brainstorming and assist when necessary.

CONTENTS

Become a Maker 4

Imagine a Robo Pet 6

Bring Your Robo Pet to Life 8

Gather Your Materials 10

Build Your Robo Pet's Body 12

What Will Your Robo Pet Do? 14

Connect Your Robo Pet 18

Decorate Your Robo Pet 20

Helpful Hacks 22

Get Inspired 24

Problem-Solve 26

Collaborate 28

The World Is a Makerspace! 30

Glossary 32

BECOME A MAKER

A makerspace is like a laboratory. It's a place where ideas are formed and problems are solved. Kids like you create amazing things in makerspaces. Many makerspaces are in schools and libraries. But they can also be in kitchens, bedrooms, and backyards. Anywhere can be a makerspace when you use imagination, inspiration, **collaboration**, and problem-solving!

IMAGINATION

This takes you to new places and lets you experience new things. Anything is possible with imagination!

INSPIRATION

This is the spark that gives you an idea. Inspiration can come from almost anywhere!

MAKERSPACE TOOLBOX

COLLABORATION

Makers work together. They ask questions and get ideas from everyone around them. **Collaboration** solves problems that seem impossible.

PROBLEM-SOLVING

Things often don't go as planned when you're creating. But that's part of the fun! Find creative **solutions** to any problem that comes up. These will make your project even better.

IMAGINE A ROBO PET

DISCOVER AND EXPLORE

Robo pets can have all kinds of cool robot features, including sounds, lights, and motion. You may have seen robo pets in movies and TV shows. You can also explore real-life robo pets on the internet. Which robo pets do you like best? What do you like about them?

GET INSPIRED!
See page 24

IMAGINE

If you could have any animal as a robo pet, what would it be? An alligator? A dolphin? Or would it be a combination of many different animals? Remember, there are no rules! Let your imagination run wild!

7

BRING YOUR ROBO PET TO LIFE

It's time to turn your dream robo pet into a makerspace marvel! What did you like most about your dream robo pet? Did it have gears, springs, and wires? Did it walk, bark, or chase its tail? How could you use the materials around you to create these features? Where would you begin?

INSPIRATION

WowWee is a company that **designs** robotic toys, such as robo pets. In 2016, the company **introduced** a robot dog, CHiP. CHiP can be controlled using certain **smartphones**. It can answer to its own name and various commands. CHiP can sit, fetch, and jump!

COLLABORATE!
See page 28

BE SAFE, BE RESPECTFUL

MAKERSPACE ETIQUETTE

THERE ARE JUST A FEW RULES TO FOLLOW WHEN YOU ARE BUILDING YOUR ROBO PET:

1. **ASK FOR PERMISSION AND ASK FOR HELP.** Make sure an adult says it's OK to make your robo pet. Get help when using sharp tools, such as scissors, or hot tools, like a glue gun.

2. **BE NICE.** Share supplies and space with other makers.

3. **THINK IT THROUGH.** Don't give up when things don't work out exactly right. Instead, think about the problem you are having. What are some ways to solve it?

4. **CLEAN UP.** Put materials away when you are finished working. Find a safe space to store unfinished projects until next time.

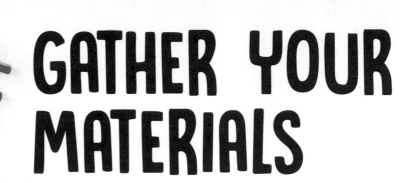

GATHER YOUR MATERIALS

Every makerspace has different supplies. Gather the materials that will help you build the robo pet of your dreams!

STRUCTURE

These are the main materials you will use to build your robo pet's body.

CONNECTING

These are the materials you will use to hold your robo pet together.

DECORATIONS & DETAILS

These are the materials you will use to make your robo pet look cool and bring it to life!

ROBOTICS

These are the materials you can use to give your robo pet a cool robotic function! They include wires, motors, and **batteries**.

COLLABORATE!
See page 28

⚠ STUCK?

LOOK BEYOND THE USUAL CRAFT SUPPLIES! THE PERFECT SHAPE MIGHT BE IN YOUR KITCHEN CABINET, GARAGE, OR TOY CHEST. SEARCH FOR MATERIALS THAT MIGHT SEEM SURPRISING.

BUILD YOUR ROBO PET'S BODY

Every structure is made up of different shapes. How can you put shapes together to make your dream robo pet?

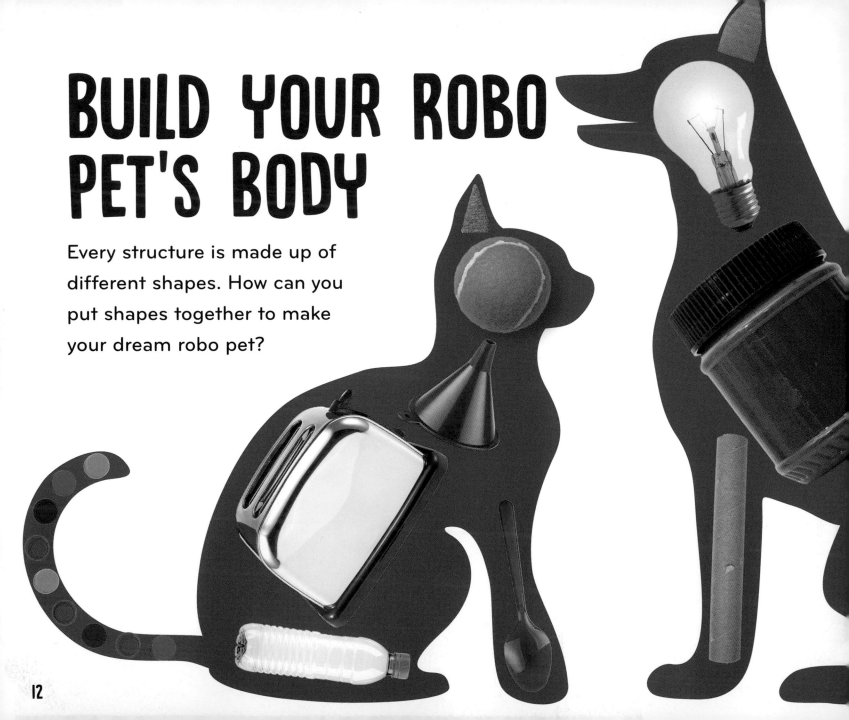

INSPIRATION

A circuit is a closed loop through which electricity can travel. Electricity moves from the power source to the load through a conductor. A switch connects and breaks the flow of electricity.

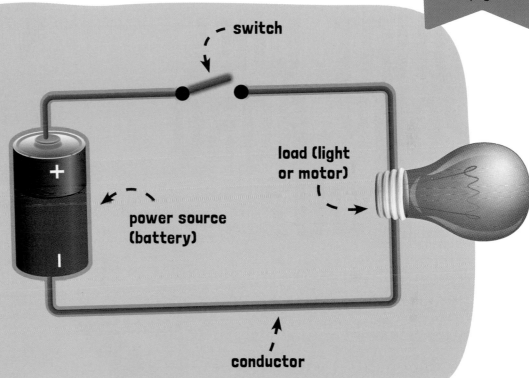

switch

load (light or motor)

power source (battery)

conductor

⚠ STUCK?

IT CAN BE USEFUL TO ASSEMBLE ANY ELECTRONIC PART OF YOUR ROBO PET FIRST. IF YOU'RE USING A CIRCUIT, BUILD IT AND MAKE SURE IT WORKS. THEN CREATE YOUR ROBO PET'S BODY TO FIT AROUND IT!

WHAT WILL YOUR ROBO PET DO?

What robotic features will your robo pet have? Knowing this will help you figure out what materials you could use to construct your robo pet.

Will it purr? Then you need a motor that **vibrates**.

PROBLEM-SOLVE!
See page 26

Dogs wag their tails to communicate emotions. What other animals move their tails?

Will it wag its tail?

Then find a motor that spins.

IMAGINE

WHAT NAME WOULD YOU GIVE YOUR ROBO PET?

15

Beginning in 1977, Tony Harding was a visual effects **designer** for the British TV series *Doctor Who*. Harding designed the show's famous robo pet, K9. The original K9 had a wagging tail, light-up eyes, and rotating ears!

Will it light up?

Then use LEDs for eyes or other flashing features.

LEDs are devices that give off light when electricity passes through them.

COLLABORATE!
See page 28

Will it look like a machine?

Then find shiny materials, such as wires, springs, and nails, for decoration.

⚠ STUCK?

YOU CAN ALWAYS CHANGE YOUR MIND IN A MAKERSPACE. DOES YOUR MOTOR SOUND MORE LIKE A BUZZ THAN A PURR? COULD YOU MAKE YOUR ROBO PET INTO AN ANIMAL THAT BUZZES INSTEAD, LIKE A BEE?

CONNECT YOUR ROBO PET

Will your robo pet be **permanent**? Or will you take it apart when you are finished? Knowing this will help you decide what materials to use.

TOTALLY **TEMPORARY**

BRASS FASTENERS   **CLOTHESPINS**   **STRAIGHT PINS**   **POSTER PUTTY**

PROBLEM—SOLVE!
See page 26

IMAGINE

WHAT IF YOU PACKED UP YOUR ROBO PET FOR A TRIP AROUND THE WORLD? HOW COULD YOU DISASSEMBLE AND REBUILD IT DURING TRAVEL?

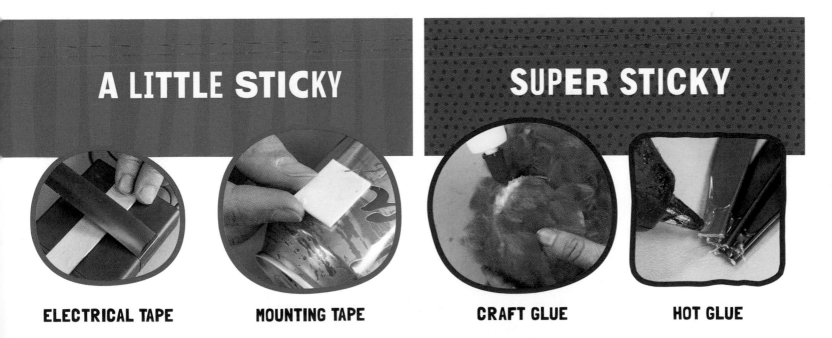

A LITTLE STICKY

ELECTRICAL TAPE

MOUNTING TAPE

SUPER STICKY

CRAFT GLUE

HOT GLUE

DECORATE YOUR ROBO PET

Decorating is the final step in making your robo pet. It's where you add **details** to your robo pet. How do your decorations bring your robo pet to life?

FELT

LEDs

SPRINGS

GET INSPIRED!
See page 24

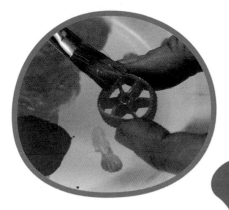

NOODLES

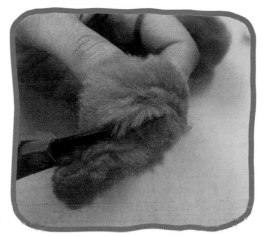

POM-POMS

PLASTIC KNIVES

CHENILLE STEMS

IMAGINE

WHAT IF YOUR ROBO PET
WERE BUILT TO PROTECT YOU?
WHAT FEATURES COULD IT HAVE
TO SCARE AWAY ENEMIES?

HELPFUL HACKS

As you work, you might discover ways to make challenging tasks easier. Try these simple tricks and **techniques** as you construct your robo pet!

The tab of a soda can is a natural connector.

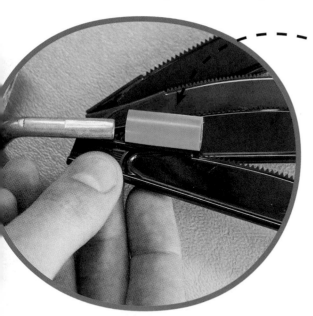

Attach straw pieces to wings so wings can slide on and off the body.

Turn a paper plate inside out to make a shell.

PROBLEM-SOLVE!
See page 26

Wrap wire around objects to secure them in place.

Use a spring and nail for the neck to allow the head to move.

Use toothpicks to piece together different body parts.

⚠ STUCK?

MAKERS AROUND THE WORLD SHARE THEIR PROJECTS ON THE INTERNET AND IN BOOKS. IF YOU HAVE A MAKERSPACE PROBLEM, THERE'S A GOOD CHANCE SOMEONE ELSE HAS ALREADY FOUND A SOLUTION. SEARCH THE INTERNET OR LIBRARY FOR HELPFUL ADVICE AS YOU MAKE YOUR PROJECTS!

GET INSPIRED

Get inspiration from the real world before you start building your robo pet!

LOOK AT ROBOTS

Many engineering companies are building robots today. Look at images of various robots. What features do they have in common? How can you create similar features in your robo pet?

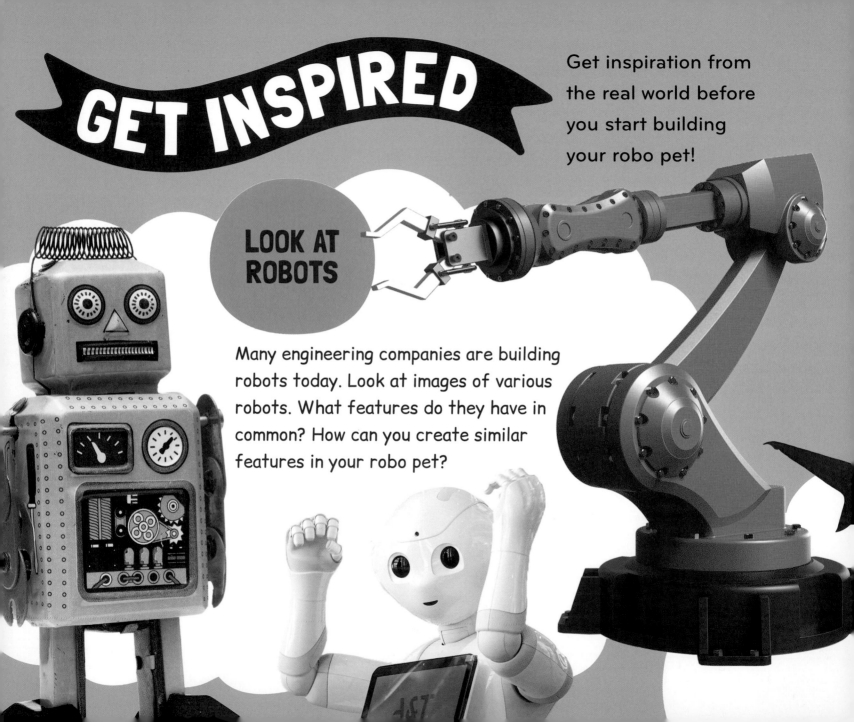

LOOK AT ART

Many artists use robotic themes in their work. Search the internet for robot art and see what you find. What materials did the artists use?

LOOK AT NATURE

Robo pets are based on real animals. Look around at the animals in your backyard or at the zoo. Which animals would be cool pets? How could you give them a robotic look?

25

PROBLEM-SOLVE

No makerspace project goes exactly as planned. But with a little creativity, you can find a **solution** to any problem.

FIGURE OUT THE PROBLEM

Maybe your robo bird's wings keep falling off its body. Why do you think this is happening? Thinking about what may be causing the problem can lead you to a solution!

SOLUTION:
Use poster putty to fill in the gap between the straw and the bird's skeleton.

SOLUTION:
Use narrower straws that fit more securely around the bird's skeleton.

BRAINSTORM AND TEST

Try coming up with three possible **solutions** to any problem.
Maybe your robo dog's tail isn't spinning along with the motor.
You could:

1. Remove any surrounding material that might be preventing the tail from spinning.

2. Use a weaker **battery** so the motor spins more slowly.

3. Attach the tail to the motor with a stronger connector, such as hot glue.

Test all three and see which works best!

ADAPT

Still stuck? Try a different material or change the **technique** slightly.

COLLABORATE

Collaboration means working together with others. There are tons of ways to collaborate to build a robo pet!

ASK A FELLOW MAKER

Talk to a friend, classmate, or family member. Other makers can help you think through the different steps to building a robo pet. These helpers can also lend a pair of hands during construction!

ASK AN ADULT HELPER

This could be a teacher, librarian, grandparent, or any trusted adult. Describe what you want a material to do instead of asking for a specific material. Your helper might think of items you didn't know existed!

ASK AN EXPERT

A veterinarian or other animal expert could share their knowledge of different animals and their behaviors. An electrician or engineer could talk to you about electronics and robotics!

THE WORLD IS A MAKERSPACE!

Your robo pet may look finished, but don't close your makerspace toolbox yet. Think about what would make your robo pet better. What would you do differently if you built it again? What would happen if you used different **techniques** or materials?

DON'T STOP AT ROBO PETS

You can use your makerspace toolbox beyond the makerspace! You might use it to accomplish everyday tasks, such as training a pet or fixing your bike. But makers use the same toolbox to do big things. One day, these tools could help care for sick people or write new laws. Turn your world into a makerspace! What problems could you solve?

GLOSSARY

battery – a small container filled with chemicals that makes electrical power.

collaborate – to work with others.

design – to plan how something will appear or work. A designer is someone who creates a sketch or outline of something that will be made.

detail – a small part of something.

expert – a person who is very knowledgeable about a certain subject.

introduce – to present or announce something new.

permanent – meant to last for a very long time.

smartphone – a cell phone that can connect to the internet and perform other computer functions.

solution – an answer to, or a way to solve, a problem.

technique – a method or style in which something is done.

vibrate – to make very small, quick movements back and forth.